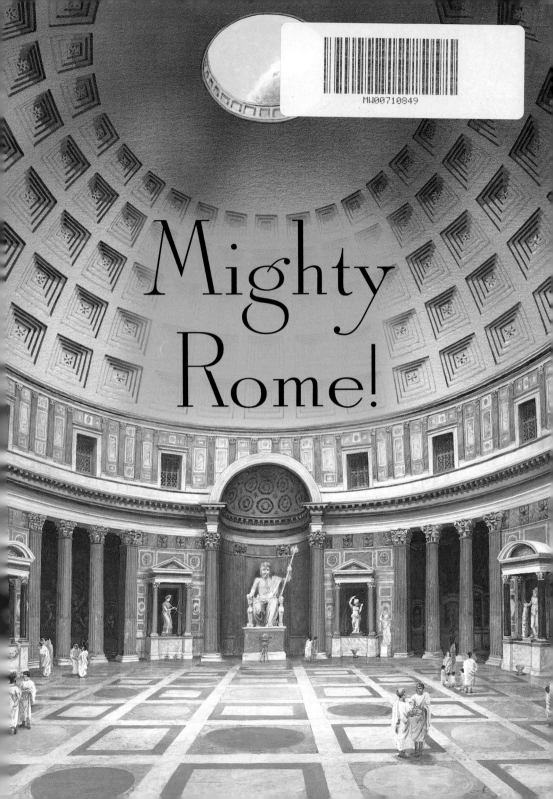

Mighty Rome!

Contents

Features

What language was used in the Roman Empire? Find out if this language is still used today on page 7.

Around 300,000 men were in the Roman army. To find out how the soldiers were organized, turn to page 18.

Discover the fashion secrets of the Romans on page 24.

Learn who attacked and robbed Rome on page 29.

Who built the city of Rome?
Visit www.rigbyinfoquest.com
for more about ROME.

The Eternal City

Rome is the capital city of Italy, in Europe. It is also one of the world's great historic cities. For over 2,000 years, Rome has been a model of **civilization.** For hundreds of years, leaders in Rome ruled the ancient Western World, known as the **Roman Empire.** Rome's importance has been so long-lasting that it is sometimes called the Eternal City.

Today, thousands of visitors travel to Rome every year to see its many monuments, churches, palaces, art museums, open-air markets, and beautiful parks and squares.

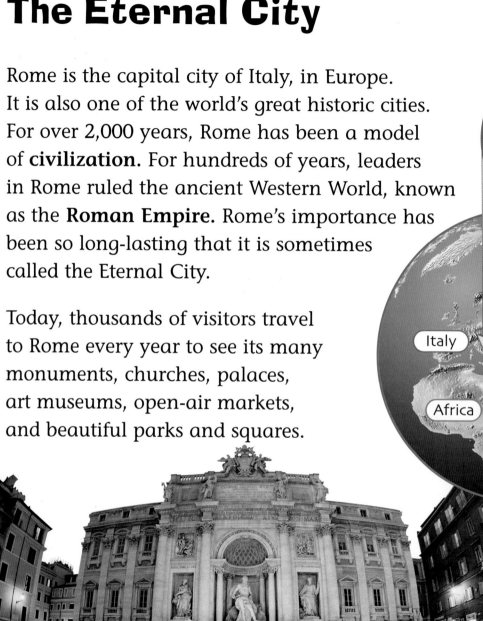

Italy

Africa

Rome

Europe

SITESEEING · MYTH & MYSTERY ·

Who built the city of Rome?

Visit **www.rigbyinfoquest.com**

for more about ROME.

The Roman Empire

At the peak of its power, the Roman Empire covered about half of Europe, much of what is now the Middle East, and the north coast of Africa. Between 50 to 70 million people lived within its borders. Nearly 1 million of these people lived in the city of Rome. This made Rome the largest city of its time.

Britain

The people of the Roman Empire spoke many languages and had different ways of life and religions. However, under Roman rule, they followed the same systems of law and government.

| Rome began over 2,750 years ago. | For the first 200 years, it was ruled by kings. | For the next 500 years, it was a **republic.** | Then Rome was the center of the Roman Empire for over 500 years. |

Ancient Europe

• Rome

Africa

Ancient Egypt

WORD BUILDER

Latin was the official language of the Roman Empire. As Roman soldiers and traders moved to new areas, the language spread. Latin is hardly ever spoken today, but our alphabet and about half of all English words come from the Latin language.

Roads and Travel

As the Roman Empire grew, roads were needed to connect towns, cities, and ports to Rome. The Roman army was given the job of building many highways. Often the soldiers had to tunnel through hills and build bridges across rivers. This work was all done by hand.

The roads they built carried soldiers, messengers, travelers, and traders about 50,000 miles across the Empire. On long journeys, travelers slept in their carriages, in tents by the roadside, or at hotels called inns.

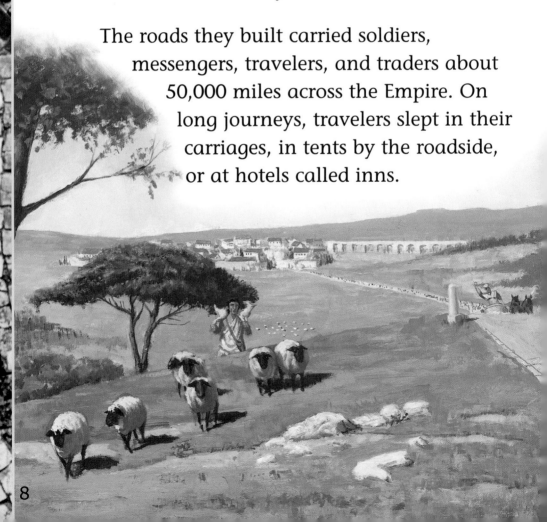

The first Roman road was
built over 2,300 years ago.
It was so well made that it is
still used today.

Roman Government

Rome was first ruled by kings. Then the people decided that they wanted to be a republic and choose their own leaders. Each year, the Roman people voted for two leaders. This system was set up so that Rome would not be ruled by just one person. It lasted for nearly 500 years.

FAST FACTS

Roman emperors did not wear crowns. They wore a wreath of laurel leaves instead. These had once been given to generals when they won battles.

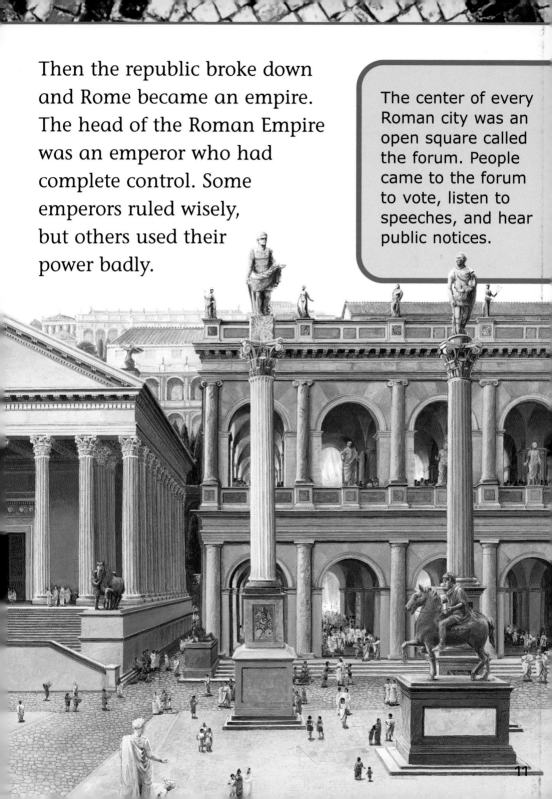

Then the republic broke down and Rome became an empire. The head of the Roman Empire was an emperor who had complete control. Some emperors ruled wisely, but others used their power badly.

The center of every Roman city was an open square called the forum. People came to the forum to vote, listen to speeches, and hear public notices.

Fighting Force

For Rome to take over more land and continue to grow, it needed a powerful army. At first, only men who owned property were allowed to be soldiers. But when more soldiers were needed, the rules were changed. Many men wanted to join the army because soldiers were fed and paid. Usually, around 300,000 men were in the Roman army at one time. These soldiers were well-trained and highly organized.

Soldiers marched long distances. They were expected to march 22 miles in five hours, wearing their armor and carrying heavy gear.

Roman soldiers built roads, **aqueducts** (shown left), walls and arches. They also guarded the empire's borders and fought off attacking armies.

Protecting the Empire

It was not enough for the Roman army to take over new territories. They also had to guard their borders and train soldiers for the next attack.

Soldiers lived in military centers called forts. A fort contained sleeping and eating quarters for the officers and the soldiers. It also contained a hospital, training halls, workshops, a bathhouse, food storage areas, and stables for the **cavalry's** horses. Small towns grew near the forts. Some of these towns are still around today.

In the time of the Roman Empire, cities were built on top of cliffs or surrounded by high stone walls. This helped to keep enemies out. However, Roman soldiers were experts at finding ways into cities. They built tall towers called siege towers and climbed up inside them so they could lower drawbridges over city walls. They used **catapults** and **battering rams** to smash their way through the walls.

The people inside the cities fought back with arrows and rocks. They set fire to the towers and poured boiling oil on the soldiers coming over the walls. In spite of this, the Roman army often got through!

When attacking, the Roman army grouped themselves together and covered the group with their shields. This kept them protected from arrows and rocks.

In the year 72, around 20,000 Roman soldiers attacked the mountain fortress of Masada in what is now Israel. The soldiers carried all their food, water, and wood across the desert, and then pitched camps around the rock. After eight months of attacking, the Romans broke through the fortress walls and took over Masada.

At the Races

The ancient Romans fought hard. They played hard, too. On public holidays, many people went to huge stadiums to watch plays, fierce battles, or **chariot** races. These events were paid for by the emperor.

The chariot teams of Rome were the Blues, Greens, Reds, and Whites. In a race, up to twelve chariots ran seven laps of the racetrack, a total of about 5 miles. People followed their favorite teams and drivers closely. Sometimes fights broke out between the fans of the different teams.

The Colosseum was the most famous stadium in the city of Rome. It seated about 50,000 people. Today, thousands of people visit the ruins of the Colosseum every year.

IN FOCUS

Dividing the Team

The Roman army was split up into sixty groups called legions. Each legion had 5,000 soldiers who were divided into ten groups called cohorts. Cohorts were split into groups of 100 men, called centuries. Centuries were then divided into small groups of men who shared a tent and ate together.

Cohort

18

On the Move

When the Roman army was marching into new areas, they had to make a camp every night. The camp was always set up in the same way so that it could be built quickly. The soldiers took turns keeping watch from lookout towers. If the enemy attacked, the army was ready to leap into action.

21

City Life, Country Life

Roman cities had offices, law courts, temples, shops, public bathhouses, and theaters. They even had aqueducts to bring in water and sewers to remove waste. Cities were crowded and many people lived in cramped conditions. Most apartments had no kitchens. People bought hot food from take-out shops or cooked in their apartments on small stoves.

Large farms throughout the Empire produced food for the army and people living in the cities. Grain was grown in Egypt and North Africa, olive oil was produced in Spain, and woolen goods in Britain. Wealthy landowners usually lived in the city but kept large homes in the country for vacations. Farm work was done by farm managers and slaves. Oxen and cattle pulled plows, and donkeys and mules were used for other work. Sheep and goats were kept for wool and milk.

23

Living with the Family

Families in ancient Rome were often large. Many children went to private schools or did lessons at home. They learned reading, writing, and math. When lessons were finished, children played with dolls, carts, and board games. They also had family pets.

FAST FACTS

In ancient Rome, everyone wore dresses! Women, children, and some men wore plain gowns called **tunics.** In the city, most men wore **togas.** Children were given special necklaces that were believed to keep them safe.

Children had to grow up more quickly than they do today. Girls got married when they were 13 or 14 years old. Their parents chose who they would marry and when the marriage would take place!

Bathtime!

Only the wealthy could afford their own bathrooms in ancient Rome. Most people who lived in the towns and cities used large public bathhouses. These bathhouses were not only for keeping clean, they also contained gardens, gymnasiums, massage rooms, libraries, meeting halls, and theaters. The local bathhouse was a popular meeting place.

Bathhouses were often beautiful buildings with marble floors and columns, painted ceilings, and statues. Roman emperors paid for the building of the bathhouses, and adults paid a small fee for using them. Children bathed for free.

The city of Bath is in southwestern England. It is famous for its natural hot spring water. The Romans built bathhouses there. Today, tourists travel to Bath to see the Roman buildings.

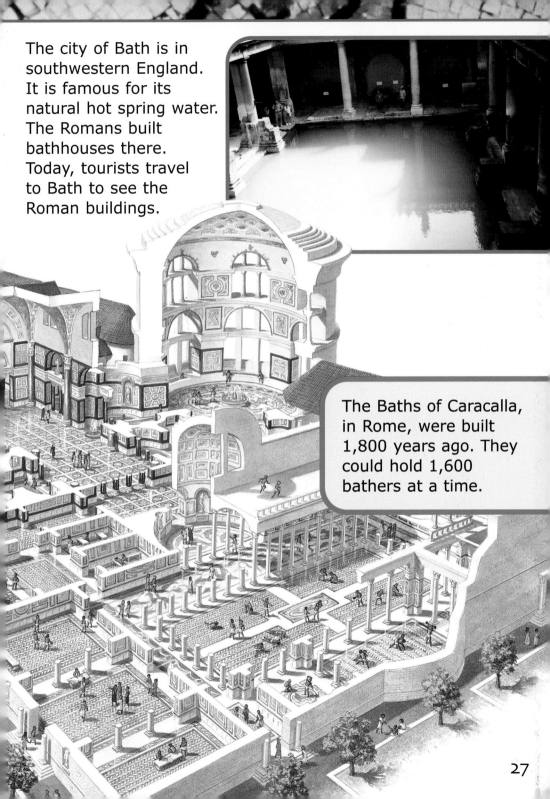

The Baths of Caracalla, in Rome, were built 1,800 years ago. They could hold 1,600 bathers at a time.

The Fall of Rome

After 500 mighty years, the Roman Empire lost its power and wealth. It had become too large and costly to run, and the army could no longer keep out attacking forces.

However, Rome's importance survives to this day. Many of the world's languages, law courts, and building designs are based on those of ancient Rome. Today, 2.7 million people live in the city of Rome—once the home of the most powerful empire in the world!

TIME LINK

A German army named the Vandals attacked the city of Rome in the year 455. In twelve days, the Vandals destroyed many books and pieces of art. They stripped Rome of everything valuable, even taking the golden roof tiles off important buildings.

Glossary

aqueduct – a channel built for moving water across long distances. Aqueduct bridges carry water over valleys and rivers.

battering ram – a heavy wooden beam used to break down an enemy's walls

catapult – a large weapon that worked like a slingshot to throw arrows, spears, or rocks

cavalry – a group of soldiers who fought on horseback

chariot – an open cart with two wheels that was pulled by horses

civilization – a highly developed and organized society with written language, arts, sciences, and government

republic – a nation in which the people choose the leaders who will make laws and run the government

Roman Empire – a group of countries under Roman rule. The Roman Empire was ruled by the emperor of Rome.

toga – a loose piece of clothing made from a length of woolen cloth. Most men wore a plain white toga, government officials wore a white toga with purple edging, and the emperor wore a purple toga.

tunic – a loose piece of clothing, like a dress, that was worn in ancient Rome. Tunics were drawn in at the waist with a belt or cord.

Index

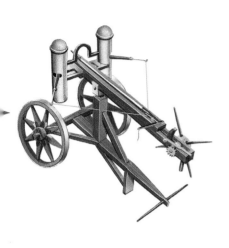

Discussion Starters

1 Have you ever heard the saying "All roads lead to Rome"? What do you think this saying means? Can you invent a saying to do with Rome for your class to use?

2 In Roman times, parents chose who their children would marry. What would be good about this? What would be bad?

3 The Vandals destroyed many things when they attacked the city of Rome. Today, we use the word *vandal* to describe a person who purposely damages or destroys other people's things. What are some examples of vandalism? Can you think of ways to stop people from becoming vandals?